The Great Irish Famine

Words and images from the Famine Museum
Strokestown Park, County Roscommon

In memory of Denis Clark (1927-93)

First published in 1994
Reprinted 1995

ISBN 0 9523541 1 X

Copyright © 1994 Stephen Campbell
Published by The Famine Museum

Designed by Kevin Boyle

Printed in Ireland by Colour Books

Special thanks to The Westward Group, Strokestown;
Pat Murphy; Hildi Hawkins; Kevin Whelan; Cormac Ó Gráda;
Orna Hanly; Josie Clark; Nick Robinson; Sean Sexton;
Jim Reynolds; Andrew Campbell; Robert Towers;
The Department of Irish Folklore, University College Dublin;
National Gallery and the staff of the National Library.

The Great Irish Famine

Words and images from the Famine Museum
Strokestown Park, County Roscommon

Stephen J. Campbell

Contents

Famine Museum

Preface

Every country is quick to make a record of its triumphs. Most cultures are rich in the lore and anecdote which celebrate heroism and strength. Reading through this book, it strikes me how important it is to make a record of a darker past as well. There are grim statistics and painful details here. They give an account of a terrible time; they illuminate the defenceless suffering of the Irish people at that time. But they serve another purpose as well: they invite us to look steadily at a past we can neither share nor change. With all its pain and disorder, the past has constructed us in the actual and literal ways of generation and inheritance. Now, if we look at it thoughtfully and clearly, and with the factual assistance of this book and the Famine Museum, that past has the power to do something more: it can construct and strengthen our understanding and our sympathy in the present.

More than anything else, this Famine Museum shows us that history is not about power and triumph nearly so often as it is about suffering and vulnerability. Those who have worked on this book and who have developed the project of this museum have done us all a true service: while these things demonstrate that the Famine is a central part of our past, that it is a motif of powerlessness which runs through our national consciousness, it is also a human drama upon which we, as Irish people, place an enormous value, and by which we have been radically instructed. As we go through the Famine Museum we have to wonder again and again at the strength of a people who could survive natural disaster and historic setback.

As we look at these artefacts and open our minds to these stories, we can feel again that it is an Irish strength to celebrate the people in our past, not for power, not for victory, but for the profound dignity of human survival. We can honour that survival best, it seems to me, by taking our folk-memory of this catastrophe into the present world with us, and allowing it to strengthen and deepen our identity with those who are still suffering.

Mary Robinson
President of Ireland

'The poor of the world today, like the poor of Europe in previous centuries, come alive for us only if we see them through the eyes of the dominant classes... They are only allowed to be interviewed, photographed, measured, weighed, analyzed, and to give a factual account of their work, their daily lives, what they eat, drink and desire. Civil servants define their basic needs in terms of calories, proteins, and lengths of cloth. They are advised to have fewer children and to educate them according to our own standards; they are urged to become more enterprising.'

Pierre Spitz, 'Silent Violence: famine and inequality',
Revue Internationale des Sciences Sociales, Vol.x (1978), No. 4.

The land and its owners before 1845

The Irish House of Commons in session, 1790

In Ireland in the nineteenth century, wealth and political power rested with those who owned the land. The great majority of the population, living mostly in the country rather than in towns, occupied land belonging to the landed gentry and paid rent for their houses and farms. Landlords lived mainly off the income from their estates and in some cases this income was invested in farming improvements. Some rich tradesmen, and a few landlords, also put money into industry – chiefly linen, and mainly in the north of the country. Many landlords lived extravagantly, and left huge debts and financial responsibilities for maintaining widows, unmarried daughters and other dependents. These accumulated debts and family settlements – or 'encumbrances' – had the effect of making each succeeding generation less wealthy.

Although subject to the British Crown, Ireland had maintained its own parliament before 1800. The assembly, which sat at College Green in Dublin during the eighteenth century, consisted mainly of landlords. Irish members of Parliament were predominately Church of Ireland Protestants whose families had settled in Ireland during the colonisations of the seventeenth century. Among these were the Mahons of Strokestown, established in Roscommon during the Cromwellian settlement of the 1650s. Catholics and, to a lesser extent, dissenters (non Church of Ireland Protestants) were barred from public office and from representation in Parliament. Laws which had restricted the right of Catholics to own land (the Penal Laws) had, however, been allowed to lapse by the late eighteenth century. Catholics with a property of a certain value were granted the right to vote in 1793.

Between 1720 and 1782, the British Parliament maintained the right to legislate for Ireland. However, the independent Dublin Parliament was able to pass laws encouraging and protecting the Irish economy which flourished in the second half of the eighteenth century. By 1810, exports from Ireland were worth between £2 and £6 million every year. Britain's engagement in foreign wars and the expansion of its

1798 Rebellion, Ballyellis, County Wexford.

empire led to a demand for Irish grain, beef, pork, butter and livestock. About half of Irish export revenues came from the rapidly expanding cottage linen industry. Parliament passed laws to encourage tillage farming, to protect the economy from imports of corn and raw materials, to outlaw rural labour unions and secret societies, and to encourage the building and improvement of roads, canals and harbours.

The Strokestown estate of Thomas Mahon MP (1701-1782) comprised approximately nine thousand acres. Thomas was regarded as an 'improving' landlord. In the 1740s he first developed Strokestown as a market town and trading centre between Dublin and the west of Ireland. The famous agricultural reformer Arthur Young (1741-1820), who visited Strokestown in the late 1760s, commented in his book *A Tour in Ireland* (1770) on the good order of Mahon's estate. He was particularly struck by the beauty of its woodlands and the flourishing linen industry in the area. Thomas was a leading figure in the Irish House of Commons, where he held a seat from 1739 to 1782. He married his sons and daughters into some of the leading families of the county, all of whom would vote for him and pressurise their clients and tenants to do likewise (there was no secret balloting). Thomas' son Maurice and his grandsons the Lieutenant Generals Thomas and Stephen Mahon all represented the county in Parliament.

The landowners of Ireland were prosperous, confident and proud of their country, but the benefits of prosperity were not spread equally. Young and other writers regarded the plight of the Irish poor as more grievous than that of their counterparts in neighbouring countries. Thousands died from starvation and disease in the famine years of 1727-1729, 1740 and 1800, leading to a stream of emigration to British North America, chiefly of Presbyterian farmers and skilled workers.

The Irish Parliament, like its British counterpart, engaged in the patronage, favouritism and bribery through which elite society assured its continuity and control. In England, however, the Irish system was seen as having failed to maintain order and to silence radical dissent. Inspired by the same anti-monarchist and egalitarian creeds which followed the American revolution of the 1770s and culminated in the 1789 revolution in France, a number of new political organisations emerged which attacked the self-interest and corruption of the Irish Parliament. There were militant political disturbances in Ireland, and calls for greater independence from within and outside Parliament, which the British Government regarded with alarm.

Attempts to reform the Irish Parliament were unsuccessful and in 1791 the United Irishmen, a federation of Catholics and Protestants dedicated to the establishment of an independent republic in Ireland, were established in Dublin and Belfast. In 1798, the United Irishmen attempted to stage a revolution with the aid of a French invasionary force. The rebellion suffered a heavy defeat, turned into bitter local feuding and was suppressed with extreme violence by the army and the landlords' militia.

The British prime minister, William Pitt (1759-1806), was convinced that the Irish colonial ruling class had failed to provide responsible leadership and that instability in Ireland could be held in check only by complete political union with Britain. After much resistance, the Dublin parliament voted for its own abolition on the 1 August 1800. Favourable conditions under the Union and rewards such as peerages had been offered by Britain to secure support for the measure. The election of 1799 which gave Thomas Mahon of Strokestown Park his seat was a contest between supporters and opponents of the union of Ireland with Great Britain. Local landlords supported Thomas on the understanding that he would vote for the Union. Once elected, Thomas became aware that many of his constituents actually opposed the measure; to avoid offending them he withdrew from the House. At the prompting of the Lord Lieutenant (the king's representative in Ireland), and with the offer of a peerage, Thomas' father Maurice bought a Commons seat for his other son, Stephen Mahon, who voted with the Unionists. Maurice was appointed First Baron Hartland of Strokestown on 10 July 1800.

The Union coincided with and greatly exacerbated a serious decline in the Irish economy. Protective legislation was gradually removed and the textile industry was steadily undermined by cheap imports and the introduction of mechanisation in the Belfast area. The ending of the Napoleonic Wars in 1814 brought widespread economic depression throughout Europe, and a falling demand for Irish agricultural products left many farmers bankrupt. The improved roads and canals established under the protectionist government of the eighteenth century now enabled the growth of monopoly producers and the easy transportation of cheaper foreign imports. Around 1800 there were three breweries in Strokestown. 'Their discontinuance', wrote Isaac Weld in his *Statistical Survey of Roscommon* (1832), 'may be attributed... to the facility with which strong beer is conveyed from Dublin, by the canal, to Tarmonbarry.'

Lord Hartland remained in residence at Strokestown, expanding his country house and implementing a new and grandiose design for the demesne. He also re-developed and expanded the town – an ambitious formal scheme with little parallel in the west of Ireland at that time. This work, undertaken in the spirit of late eighteenth century economic optimism, involved huge expenditure, nearly all of which was borrowed.

With Maurice's death in 1819 the title was inherited by his son Thomas, and after Thomas' death in 1835 by another son, also named Maurice. Maurice suffered from a mental disorder and in 1836 a special inquiry of the Court of Chancery declared him unfit to manage his affairs. He was made a ward of the Court, which became responsible for administering the estate. His capital was made inaccessible to other members of the family and when Maurice died in 1845 the estate had suffered from ten years of neglect. The title expired with Maurice, who was succeeded by his cousin Major Denis Mahon (1787-1847) in the year in which the potato blight struck in Ireland for the first time.

'The swinish multitude'

IRISH BOG TROTTERS.

'Throughout Connaught a large portion of the estates remain in the hands of families who have possessed them for centuries; but their real value has long since been obtained and spent by the predecessors of the present nominal owners. The relation between landlord and tenant is, in truth, lost; in no country in the world are these duties less recognised than in Ireland... The embarrassed landlord has, of course, no money to expend upon improvements; his apparent interest is to extort the highest possible rent from the estate... The estates in Chancery are notoriously ill-managed and neglected. The only power which appears to be exercised by this court is that of exacting the uttermost farthing of rent. The tenants in consequence become degraded, and, left to themselves, let and sublet, to their own great injury and that of the estate.'

James Hack Tuke, *Transactions during the Famine in Ireland, 1846-1847.*

'It will be difficult for most of our readers to feel near akin with a class which at best wallows in pigsties and hugs the most brutish degradation. But when we take the sum of the British people, the "ill fed ill clothed ill honoured" children of the Celt count with Victoria's own children.'

The Times (London) 3 January 1848.

Now that the British Government had become directly responsible for Ireland, it undertook a series of investigations into the state of the country – population censuses, reports on the condition of landed property, a survey of poverty, and an ordnance survey of the entire country. The results were alarming. The government became uncomfortably aware of the hundreds of thousands of landless and destitute poor. This population of 'paupers' was seen as a threat to social stability and an obstacle to any economic prosperity. This under-class was also regarded as a dangerously mobile population. The large-scale migration of Irish labourers to Britain to seek employment was a well-established practice prior to the nineteenth century. The thousands of Irish poor who flocked to England and Scotland every year for seasonal employment were seen as a menace, a kind of social disease which would 'infect' both public health and public morality. The annual 'droves' or 'swarms' of migrant workers were seen, by the 1830s, as taking jobs from the indigenous labour force and were also regarded as having an undesirable effect 'on the moral character of the natives'. According to an 1836 report, their influence was of a 'mischievous description' and damaging to the 'superior character of the Scotch and English poor'. The authors of the various surveys frequently pointed out causes for such social ills but there was strong opposition to doing anything for Ireland. The Irish poor were perceived as being of a different and degenerate race and religion, and no class existed in England of a level of poverty comparable to the Irish rural labourer.

According to the 1841 Census, there were 8,175,124 people living in Ireland. This figure indicated an increase of 175 per cent since 1780, making Ireland one of the most densely populated countries in Europe. In Roscommon alone, the population had risen from 158,110 in 1813 to 253,491 in 1841 – an increase of 60 per cent. The Poor Inquiry of 1832 found that three million people were at poverty level. 100,000 of these were widows, orphans and unemployed in a state of total destitution requiring welfare of some kind.

With the ending of the Napoleonic Wars in 1815, the demand for Irish grain fell dramatically as Britain began to import from the continent and the rapid population increase led to heavy competition for land and to high rents. A rise in the demand for meat led to a shift from tillage to grazing and a significant decrease in the demand for farm labour. The more 'progressive' landlords and middlemen sought to clear their estates of impoverished smallholders, re-dividing land into cattle-pastures in Leinster and Munster and 'sheep-walks' in east Connacht.

In the wake of the Act of Union, landlords resided at their country estates less and less, using the rental income to support political careers or fashionable living in England. Their estates were frequently let on long leases at low rent to wealthy farmers known as middlemen who made vast profits by sub-letting at increased rents to numerous under-tenants. Middlemen usually cared little for the effective overall management of the landlord's property. Leases to middlemen were usually negotiated on a townland basis, with the middleman, in turn, allocating rental responsibilities within the community. This system saved the landlord the trouble of dealing with a multiplicity of small, fractious leaseholders, leaving the resident middleman to deal with such contentious issues as the regulation of communal grazing, the fixing of rents, and the allocation of strips of land. For the tenant this arrangement afforded a good degree of protection from rack-renting and the competition for land.

The very poor held land in one of two ways. The 'cottier' was a farm labourer who rented a small portion of land annually from his employer. The cottier paid rent by working a fixed number of days on the employer's farm. This arrangement was more common in Leinster than Connacht. In Connacht the 'conacre' system was more prevalent. A casual or seasonal labourer made an annual arrangement to occupy a portion of manured ground to grow one year's crop of potatoes. Rents were sometimes more than twice what would have been payable on leased holdings.

In the west of the country there was always strong competition for land between large-scale grazers and small-scale tillage farmers. To improve their bargaining power, small farmers often formed a collective or partnership to bid for a townland lease. They were able to outbid the grazers on the poorer ground, which was unsuitable for large-scale cattle ranching. These partnership tenants often lived in clusters of houses (called villages or *clachans*), pooling their resources and practising a communal style of farming known as rundale. These clustered settlements represented a sophisticated environmental response to the farming of marginal lands, and were very successful in reclaiming bog and mountain areas. The practice was sometimes encouraged by landlords as land reclamation works increased the value of their property. As the population grew, these clusters swelled rapidly and the partnership 'shares' were subdivided again and again. The large-scale reclamation of waste land was made possible by intensive manual labour and the intricate system of 'lazybed' spade cultivation.

The cabin clusters which formed the nucleus of the rundale settlements were usually made of stone, had one or two rooms, and a thatched roof. Although these groupings often contained up to thirty dwellings, there were no services typical of a village such as shops, church or public-house. Each dwelling was accompanied by a heavily manured and intensively cultivated tillage plot, the 'in-field'. A communal 'out-field', separated from the 'in-field' by a stone wall, was used for pasture and turbary (the use of bog for cultivation, fuel, and fertilizer).

The highly concentrated nature of the settlement denied any division between private and public space. Much of the domestic work took place outside the cabin, which was really little more than a secure

Bridget O'Donnell and her children

The Middleman and The Strong Farmer, *Illustrated London News*

shelter from the elements. The area immediately adjoining the cabin included a conspicuous dungheap, the detritus of farming and domestic activities, and foraging pigs. The much maligned dungheap, frequently cited as an example of laziness and slovenliness, was in fact a symbol of the farmer's commitment to, and dependence on, potato cultivation: the success of the potato crop depended absolutely on the quality and quantity of manure. The dungheap was a symbol of wealth, not poverty, within the rundale system. This point was completely misunderstood by travellers ignorant of the dynamics of the rundale system. Similarly, the much maligned 'pig in the parlour', frequently cited as evidence of slovenliness, played a pivotal ecological role in this system. The potato is impossible to store over long periods, and the pig represented a very efficient means of using waste potatoes to create manure.

In Connacht, and particularly in the Strokestown area, crowded rundale townlands on poor land were to be found side-by-side with empty grazing townlands on richer soil held by middlemen. It was this highly visible form of social inequality which fuelled agrarian unrest often manifested by the 'houghing', or maiming, of cattle. According to Isaac Weld, middlemen around Strokestown were charging twice as much per acre as would have been payable to the landowner, 'so that here, as indeed in many other parts of the country, the people were anxiously waiting for the expiration of their terms under the middleman, in the confidence of receiving more favourable conditions from the lord of the soil'.

In the country as a whole, just under half of all farms were of less than five acres, and in Connacht the figure was closer to three-quarters. The expansion of rural population and the proliferation of tiny farms has traditionally been explained by, or blamed on, the farming of a single cheap, high-yielding and nutritious food staple by small farmers and labourers. But this crop, the potato, was an effect and not a cause. Irish people had been marrying young and having large families as a result of the flourishing rural economy of the late eighteenth and early nineteenth centuries, which was founded on tillage farming and the cottage linen industry. This huge rural labour force had become largely redundant by the mid-nineteenth century. As a result, the rate of population expansion was actually levelling by the 1840s. There was less incentive for people to marry young and produce large families. More people were emigrating, individually or in organised schemes.

Middlemen and 'strong farmers' with holdings of thirty acres or more who raised several crops and kept livestock were concentrated in Leinster. There they numbered almost 18,000, while less than one-quarter of that number could be found in Connacht. Most Connacht tenants held no lease – 'tenants-at-will' – and were liable to be evicted at any time. These farmers raised only grain crops and livestock to finance the payment of rent. If they were dispossessed, the landlord was not obliged to compensate them for any building, drainage or other improvements carried out on their holdings.

Spinning had given women an important role in maintaining family incomes, making survival on tiny holdings more of a possibility. In 1841, one in seven women in Connacht was active as a spinner, chiefly of woollen yarns. The cottage linen industry had collapsed by the 1830s, except where it had successfully adapted to mechanisation, as in north-east Ulster. Flax had been cultivated in great quantities around Roscommon in the early part of the nineteenth century. By 1830, only a few patches remained which did not even satisfy the moderate local demand.

By the 1840s, Ireland's economy was stagnant. Few had the means or the confidence to invest capital or effort in the countryside. Communications were poor, violence was rife, and agriculture generally undercapitalised. There was a prevailing atmosphere of bitterness and hostility between those who controlled the land – especially the middlemen – and those who worked it. By British standards, rents were high and there was heavy competition for land, which was often leased to the highest bidder. These circumstances prevented tenants from expanding and improving their farms, and led instead to increasing poverty as holdings diminished through subdivision and subletting, and this in turn engendered over-dependence on the potato. One acre of poor ground could yield six tonnes of potatoes, enough to feed six adults for a year.

Patrick Browne of Clonfad, brother of the Catholic bishop of Elphin, was typical of the middlemen of the Strokestown estate. Browne's father had held 192 acres at Clonfad since the 1760s. In 1822, a new lease was negotiated with the second Lord Hartland at a higher rent. Patrick and his son were named as partners in the lease with the elder Browne. The latter would sign only with the guarantee that the others 'would not in any manner exercise any power, authority, or title to the land during his life'. The old man then proceeded to issue sub-leases at random, without the knowledge of his son and without keeping copies. Patrick attempted to repudiate these and to re-establish the tenants in conacre, but was defeated when the tenants brought the cases to court. By 1846, there were 56 families of under tenants living on the Browne holding, many involved in the general rent strike on the Mahon estate. Patrick called upon Mahon's agent and the sheriff to have 30 families evicted in Mahon's name, despite the Major's insistence that middlemen were solely responsible for their own under tenants.

Certain Irish members of Parliament sought to improve the small farmer's lot by constitutional means, citing as exemplarary the practice of some landlords in Ulster. The reform movement envisioned the replacement of masses of leaseless labourers and tenants-at-will with a secure and legally protected tenantry. Tenants would be given incentives to improve farming methods and productivity through guarantees of fair rent, safeguards against arbitrary eviction and compensation for improvements when a tenant vacated a holding. Those who opposed the idea of tenant right argued that Ireland's problems resulted from the idleness of its population, its lack of industry and self-sufficiency. According to the Whig (Liberal) prime minister Lord John Russell (1792-1878), 'one might as well compensate rabbits for the burrows they have made'.

'Low as is the condition of the cottier or labourer, whose labour merely pays the rent of his cabin and potato-garden, there is yet a lower class; those who, having no certain employment, are obliged to pay a money rent for their wretched cabin, and for the land which they take in con-acre, and whose subsistence depends on the success of their crop. If they fail, they have no resource; their bed or whatever they have is probably distrained for the rent; nothing remains. There is so little employment to be had, that they have no alternative but to beg, or steal, or starve… The labourers who go annually to reap the harvest in England, and in the eastern parts of Ireland, are mostly of this class; and their earnings during this season of employment pay the rent of their cabin and con-acre, and assist in clothing them… There are no means of ascertaining exactly the number of persons who were dependent on conacre potatoes for their support, but it must have formed a large portion of the population of all the western counties, and was not inconsiderable even in the eastern counties of Leinster and Ulster. Perhaps it may be estimated at 2,000,000.'

Jonathan Pim, *The Condition and Prospects of Ireland*, 1848.

'The hovels which the poor people were building as I passed, solely by their own efforts, were of the most abject description; their walls were formed, in several instances, by the backs of fences; the floors sunk in the ditches; the height scarcely enough for a man to stand upright; poles not thicker than a broomstick for couples; a few pieces of grass sods the only covering; and these extending only partially over the thing called a roof; the elderly people miserably clothed; the children all but naked.'

Isaac Weld, *Statistical Survey of Roscommon*, 1832.

The coming of blight

THE REAL POTATO BLIGHT OF IRELAND.

'When earning nothing, persons who are in the habit of employing me have lent me money to be repaid in work when they would have employment for me. At such times we have lived on one meal of dry potatoes in the day. I and my four children have often lived on eight stone of potatoes for the whole week; about sixteen stone would be sufficient for us. We very seldom at any time of the year have milk with our potatoes; we sometimes have a salt herring, but we eat them three times dry for once that we have anything with them and it is not the best even of potatoes that we have. We have the cheapest and worst sort of lumpers, that we may have them plentiful. I am not able to clothe my children; the wages I can earn are too little even to buy potatoes for them; but the people that employ me… are kind enough to help me now and then with a little food or seeds beyond my wages.'

Testimony of Widow Kilboy to the commissioners of the Poor Inquiry, 1836.

'I wish there was not a tenant in Baltiboys, there will not be many by and by, no small holders at any rate. When potatoes are gone a few acres won't be worth a man's time to manage. What a revolution for good will this failure of cheap food cause.'

The Irish Journals of Elizabeth Smith, 23 September 1846.

The potato was introduced to Ireland during the colonial settlements of the late sixteenth and early seventeenth century. Sir Walter Raleigh is said to have cultivated it on his estates in County Cork in the 1580s. By 1606, it is recorded at Comber, County Down, by Scottish settlers during the Ulster plantation. It rapidly established itself as the principal food of the Irish poor, probably in response to the horrific conditions of life as the country was ravaged by the armies of James I, of Cromwell and of William III. The potato survived, concealed underground as soldiers laid the land waste, seizing or destroying cattle or grain crops. In 1662, the scientist Sir Robert Boyle reported that the potato had kept thousands alive at a time of general famine.

By the 1840s, the potato was the most extensively cultivated crop in Ireland. It accounted for just over two million statute acres (800,000ha), or one-third of all tilled land, and was the staple food of the majority of the population. By the 1840s, three million Irish consumed little else but the potato, which was used as a staple more commonly than bread among all classes of rural society. An adult rural labourer consumed as much as 14 lbs (6.3kg) of potatoes per day. Together with buttermilk, this diet provided adequate proteins, fats, carbohydrates, calcium and iron. By the 1840s, many of the poor were relying on the bland, high-yielding lumper potato variety, which had first made its appearance as an animal fodder. The more nutritious and appetizing cup and apple varieties were grown mainly for sale. The potato is rich in vitamin C, and vitamin deficiency diseases such as scurvy were rare in Ireland. Travellers in Ireland noted the healthy appearance of a people nourished almost entirely on the potato. A people described as being the most wretched in Europe were also regarded as among the best nourished, the most physically robust and the tallest.

The potato was difficult to store and to transport. About 15 per cent of the crop was lost through decay. Stocks generally lasted about ten and a half months, and the six weeks before the potato harvest were periods of hardship when people relied on scanty rations of oatmeal, eggs, herrings, or lard. Farmers and labourers in the northern counties relied on a year-round supplement of oatmeal, which had been a traditional food of Scottish planters in Ulster from the seventeenth century. During the summer months, inhabitants of the coastal counties ate herring. Other kinds of fish were transferred for sale to urban markets.

Fishing, especially on the west coast, was a seasonal activity. Fishing communities were heavily dependent on potatoes for the months of the year when the seas were not navigable. With the failure of

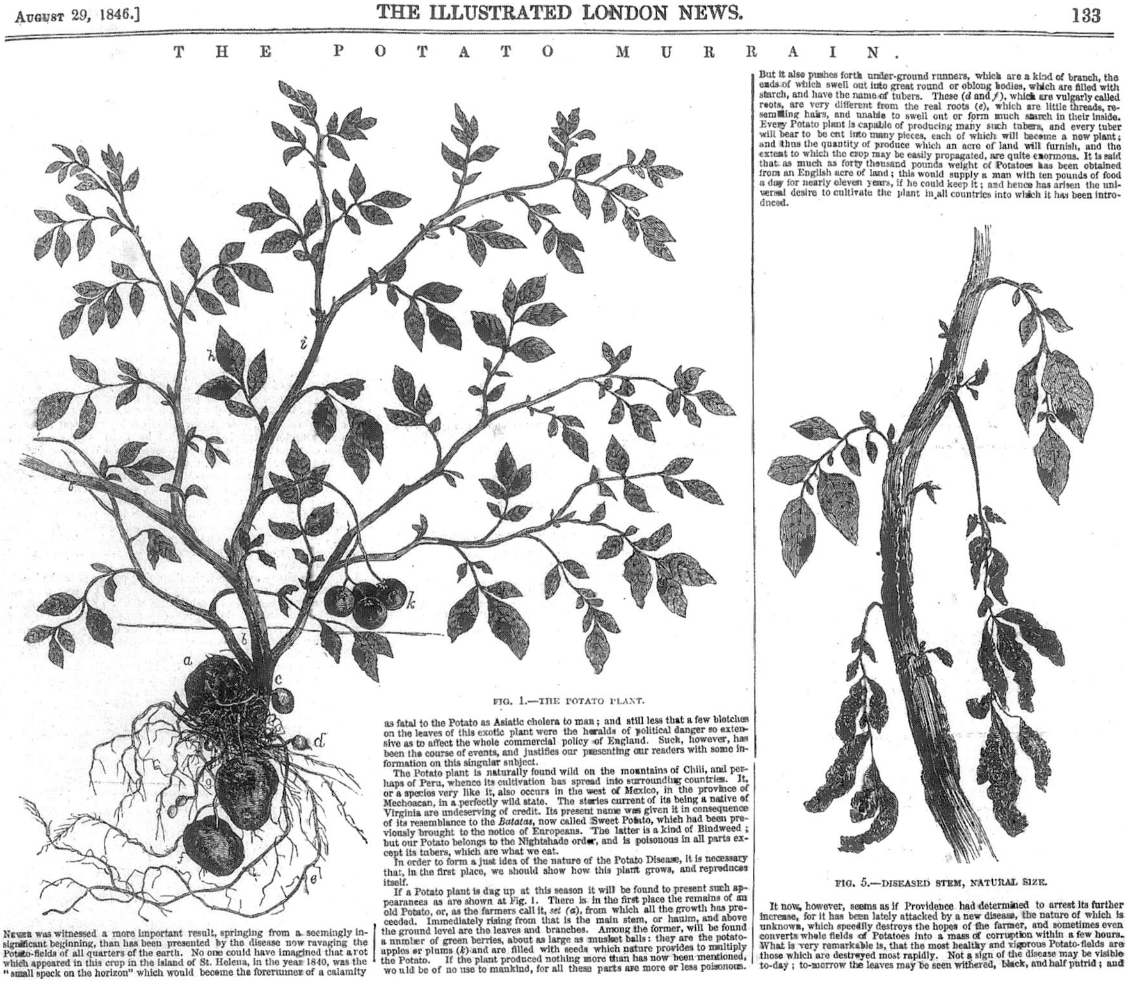

THE POTATO MURRAIN.

But it also pushes forth under-ground runners, which are a kind of branch, the ends of which swell out into great round or oblong bodies, which are filled with starch, and have the name of tubers. These (d and f), which are vulgarly called roots, are very different from the real roots (e), which are little threads, resembling hairs, and unable to swell out or form much starch in their inside. Every Potato plant is capable of producing many such tubers, and every tuber will bear to be cut into many pieces, each of which will become a new plant; and thus the quantity of produce which an acre of land will furnish, and the extent to which the crop may be easily propagated, are quite enormous. It is said that as much as forty thousand pounds weight of Potatoes has been obtained from an English acre of land; this would supply a man with ten pounds of food a day for nearly eleven years, if he could keep it; and hence has arisen the universal desire to cultivate the plant in all countries into which it has been introduced.

FIG. 1.—THE POTATO PLANT.

as fatal to the Potato as Asiatic cholera to man; and still less that a few blotches on the leaves of this exotic plant were the heralds of political danger so extensive as to affect the whole commercial policy of England. Such, however, has been the course of events, and justifies our presenting our readers with some information on this singular subject.

The Potato plant is naturally found wild on the mountains of Chili, and perhaps of Peru, whence its cultivation has spread into surrounding countries. It, or a species very like it, also occurs in the west of Mexico, in the province of Mechoacan, in a perfectly wild state. The stories current of its being a native of Virginia are undeserving of credit. Its present name was given it in consequence of its resemblance to the Batatas, now called Sweet Potato, which had been previously brought to the notice of Europeans. The latter is a kind of Bindweed; but our Potato belongs to the Nightshade order, and is poisonous in all parts except its tubers, which are what we eat.

In order to form a just idea of the nature of the Potato Disease, it is necessary that, in the first place, we should show how this plant grows, and reproduces itself.

If a Potato plant is dug up at this season it will be found to present such appearances as are shown at Fig. 1. There is in the first place the remains of an old Potato, or, as the farmers call it, set (a), from which all the growth has proceeded. Immediately rising from that is the main stem, or haulm, and above the ground level are the leaves and branches. Among the former, will be found a number of green berries, about as large as musket balls: they are the potato-apples or plums (k) and are filled with seeds which nature provides to multiply the Potato. If the plant produced nothing more than has now been mentioned, wo uld be of no use to mankind, for all these parts are more or less poisonous.

Never was witnessed a more important result, springing from a seemingly insignificant beginning, than has been presented by the disease now ravaging the Potato-fields of all quarters of the earth. No one could have imagined that a rot which appeared in this crop in the island of St. Helena, in the year 1840, was the "small speck on the horizon" which would become the forerunner of a calamity

FIG. 5.—DISEASED STEM, NATURAL SIZE.

It now, however, seems as if Providence had determined to arrest its further increase, for it has been lately attacked by a new disease, the nature of which is unknown, which speedily destroys the hopes of the farmer, and sometimes even converts whole fields of Potatoes into a mass of corruption within a few hours. What is very remarkable is, that the most healthy and vigorous Potato-fields are those which are destroyed most rapidly. Not a sign of the disease may be visible to-day; to-morrow the leaves may be seen withered, black, and half putrid; and

The potato murrain

the potato crop in late 1846, many fishermen were forced to sell their boats and tackle in order to survive during the winter, thus depriving themselves of their livelihood and major food source for the following year.

Phytophtora infestans, the fungus which invades the potato plant and causes its rapid decay, struck for the first time in the eastern United States in the summer of 1843. The invisible fungus spores were transported to Belgium in a cargo of apparently healthy potatoes, and in the summer of 1845 the fungus revived and reproduced, devastating the potato crop in Flanders, Normandy, Holland and southern England. Aware of the impending disaster should the blight spread to Ireland, the British prime minister, Robert Peel (1788-1850), ordered the Irish Constabulary to report on the state of the crop. By 20 August, blight was recorded at the Dublin Botanical Gardens by Dr David Moore (1808-1879). A week later, a total failure of the crop was reported from County Fermanagh. By October, there was panic in the west of Ireland, as the blight destroyed healthy potatoes harvested in August. Anticipating famine,

Peel organised the purchase of supplies of Indian corn (maize) from North America, repealing protectionist laws against the import of corn amid much controversy.

In November, reports from Ireland claimed that half the crop had been destroyed by the mysterious potato disease. With the onset of winter, the effects of the fungus, which reproduces in warmer conditions, were less apparent, and many believed the disaster to have ended. The poor starved themselves in order to use their food supply as seed for the following year's crop. Yet by the following February new potatoes, displayed at the London Royal Horticultural Society, showed unmistakable signs of blackening decay. A heatwave the following summer, accompanied by continual rain, provided ideal conditions for the revival of blight. Grain harvests in Ireland and throughout Europe were extremely poor, and surplus American grain was rapidly exhausted by emergency orders from other countries. By the beginning of the harsh winter of 1846, it was evident that the potato crop had been almost totally destroyed.

To the people and to the scientific experts who urgently sought a remedy, the blight was an inexplicable horror. Many saw it as the work of a supernatural influence, of evil spirits or God's curse on Ireland following the Catholic Emancipation Act (1829) or the Government's support of the establishment of a seminary at Maynooth, County Kildare. Others blamed it on the use of *guano* fertiliser, or regarded the blight as a lesson to the Irish poor against overbreeding or reliance on the 'lazy man's' crop, the potato. The official government inquiry decided that the disease was a result of wet weather which had rotted the plants. Government pamphlets instructed farmers to dry the potatoes in pits with ventilation funnels, or in ovens. Another highly impractical, expensive and dangerous proposal suggested a mixture of oil of vitriol, manganese dioxide and salt, to create chlorine gas which could then be used to treat diseased potatoes. The official pamphlets also contained complicated directions for extracting starch from diseased potatoes, to be used for bread, regardless of the lack of nutritional value. An article published in the *Gardener's Chronicle* in 1846, which suggested that the symptoms of the blight resembled the behaviour of a fungus, was dismissed or ignored. The non-acceptance of the 'fungus theory' was the main obstacle to the development of a treatment against the disease. As early as 1832, it was known that copper sulphate or bluestone had fungicidal properties, and grain with dry-rot had been treated successfully by steeping it in a solution of the compound. A correspondent in the *Gardener's Chronicle* (1846) noted that potatoes grown near a copper smelting works in Swansea remained free of the blight, but this observation met with scepticism and denial. Bluestone by itself proved to have little effect. David Moore, curator at the Dublin Botanical Gardens, tried steeping potatoes in a solution of copper sulphate in 1846, but no beneficial effects were then noted, and the possibilities of bluestone were left tragically unexplored for several decades.

In France in 1862, a bluestone solution used to treat vines for a fungal disease caused by *peronospora* proved to have a beneficial effect on diseased potatoes planted nearby. This observation led to the development of 'Bordeaux mixture' (bluestone and lime), which was sprayed on to the plant to kill the spores. The bluestone spray was not widely used in Ireland until the close of the nineteenth century, by which time *phytophtora infestans* had destroyed the crop again in 1862 and 1880.

Ireland in crisis: the beginnings of social welfare

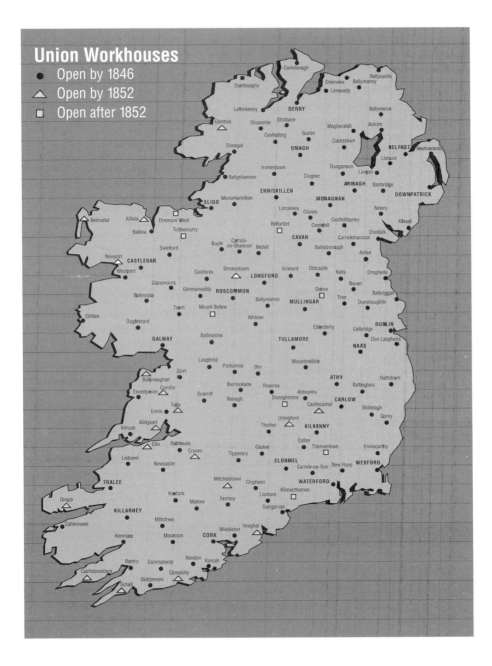

Union Workhouses
- ● Open by 1846
- △ Open by 1852
- □ Open after 1852

'Another day of bad weather yet all get out but me, sick poor, destitute poor, and ignorant, idle, prejudiced poor, oppress me. Relieve them I can't, instruct them I can't, but I can try, every little helps… Energy is so wanting among these Celtick races there is no inspiring them to help themselves, and there is no other help really availing. Mental force seems to be wanting, it will require a generation or two to reproduce any in beings so degraded. How absurd in me to feel angry with creatures so deficient yet their folly is so lamentable it is very hard to bear patiently all the evil it produces.'

The Irish Journals of Elizabeth Smith, 28 October 1845.

'And Gentlemen, you know but very little of the state of the suffering poor. If Mr Barton knew our state he should not adopt the policy of breaking 100 men more to protract work instead of giving us employment. But Gentlemen, we must cry out against the policy of protracting the work for the few, while we are suffering from famine and the want of employment… We are willing to work, and hope, Gentlemen, you will take part in remedying our present calamity by giving us employment or by getting Mr Barton to do so.'

Petition of the tenants of Cloonahee, Elphin, County Roscommon to the Strokestown Relief Committee, 22 August 1846

By the winter of 1846-47, a form of public welfare was in operation in Ireland, although it was far from adequate to deal with the millions of people requiring assistance. In the 1830s, the government had created two bodies to deal with the problem of endemic poverty in Ireland. The Irish Board of Works was set up in 1831 to improve the economy and alleviate poverty by providing employment. Under its provisions committees of local land owners – Grand Juries – were to submit proposals for road, harbour and bridge construction, or for bog clearance and drainage, with loans, grants and technical expertise from the Board.

In an attempt to restrict the migration of Irish labourers, a select committee was established in 1830 to investigate the state of the poor in Ireland and the provision of schemes to alleviate poverty. This Poor Inquiry Commission reported in 1836 that 2,385,000 people were in such a state of poverty as to require organised welfare schemes. The government responded in 1838 with a government act 'for the More Effective Relief of the Destitute Poor in Ireland', modelled on the English Poor Law system, which had been in existence since the sixteenth century.

Ireland was divided into 130 'Unions' – groups of parishes in which local property owners and rent payers of a certain valuation were obliged to pay a 'Poor Rate' towards the maintenance of the destitute poor in that area (i.e. the more prosperous the tenants, the less the land owner would have to pay). From 1843, landlords were liable for the poor rate of tenants with holdings valued at less than £4.

Although Ireland formed part of the United Kingdom, the Government saw it not as a local region for which it had direct responsibilities, but as another country ultimately accountable for its own condition and problems. Rather than seeing poverty as resulting from social inequality, or from exploitation by those who controlled the land, those responsible for relief policy were influenced by ideas of the natural superiority of rich over poor, of 'Anglo-Saxon' over 'Celt', of Protestant over Catholic. Human society was seen as a living organism in which famines occurred as natural checks to population growth. 'The great evil with which we have to contend', wrote Charles Trevelyan (1807-1886), the Treasury secretary responsible for funding government relief operations, 'is not the physical evil of famine but the moral evil of the selfish, perverse and turbulent character of the people.' Such 'naturally' lazy people would never resort to 'honest industry' and become self-sufficient if they were provided with free handouts of food at government expense. Relief was therefore made subject to arduous and humiliating conditions, taking the form of manual labour for the lowest possible wages or confinement in prison-like institutions known as workhouses.

The Linen Hall, Dublin, 1783.

London Pub.d by W. Holland N.o 50 Oxford St. February 20th 1799.

~ UNION between ENGLAND & IRELAND!!

A SKETCH OF THE GREAT AGI·TATÉR

Pub March 6 1829 by T McLean 26 Haymarket

The discovery of the potato blight in Ireland, Daniel McDonald, 1821-1853

Sir Robert Peel

An emigrant ship, Dublin bay, at sunset, Edwin Hayes

CAPTAIN ROCK'S BANDITTI SWEARING IN A NEW MEMBER

Lazy Beds, Louisburgh, County Mayo, 1992

By 1840, each Union was obliged to provide for the upkeep of its own poor in workhouses, despite the Poor Inquiry Commission's protestations that it would not be able to cope with the vast numbers of destitute and that the unemployed in Ireland did not need to be forced to work. The Union workhouses combined accommodated about 100,000 people, but by the winter of 1846-47 more than five times that number had qualified for admission. The workhouse was a complex of buildings designed to contain about one thousand 'paupers'. A pauper was defined as a person reduced to a state of 'total destitution', although this turned out to be a rather flexible classification which gave rise to much contention. Could someone with a few acres, or a 'means of livelihood' such as a horse or a cow, be considered destitute? Was it permissible for a farmer to place his wife and children in the workhouse for the winter months while he laboured for the recovery of their small farm? The 1847 Poor Law Extension Act (Gregory Clause) harshly resolved the uncertainty. Now all tenant farmers seeking admission for their families had to surrender all holdings of more than one-quarter of an acre. Although it was pointed out that it was counter-productive to reduce people to further dependency before they could receive government aid, the measure was consistent with the view of relief as punitive. When admitted, inmates were compelled to wear a regulation uniform. When the workhouse at Castlerea, County Roscommon ran out of uniforms in November 1846, applicants were repeatedly turned away until their entreaties led the Guardians to grant them admission. Because of the very basic diet and grossly inadequate hygiene standards and health care, the chance of survival of those admitted to the workhouse was greatly diminished.

Having surrendered any hope of future recovery, the inmates were subjected to further demoralisation within the workhouse through the breaking up of families. Men, women, boys and girls were housed separately. Inmates were subjected to authoritarian discipline with no provision for privacy, comfort or recreation, and with frequent punishments – dismissal for adults or flogging for children – for failure to observe the numerous rules. Food was of the cheapest kind – bread, stirabout (thin oatmeal based soup), milk and potatoes when available.

Total destitution was forestalled by many in the first year of the potato failure by Robert Peel's controversial import of corn from North America. Ground into meal, the corn was sold at a low price from depots in each county, as an economic strategem designed to keep down the price of other foodstuffs on the market. In County Roscommon, the meal was distributed in towns such as Strokestown, Boyle, Castlerea and Roscommon. The poor from smaller towns and rural areas had to walk many miles in order

Miss Kennedy distributing clothing at Kilrush, *Illustrated London News*

Government sale of Indian corn at Cork, *Illustrated London News*

to purchase a government ration, and the centralised distribution led to thousands converging on the depot towns from the surrounding areas. On 7 October 1846, cavalry and infantry had to be called in to prevent the desperate and angry crowd from breaking into the depot in Roscommon town.

In March 1846, four bills were introduced to increase employment, largely in the form of projects directed by the Board of Works. Local committees were invited to submit proposals for improvements which were to be of general public rather than of private benefit. These works chiefly took the form of road building. Later, schemes of benefit to private property were allowed subject to a contribution from the landowner. Major Denis Mahon reported in June that he expected to spend as much as £500 on new roads linking Strokestown with Carrick-on-Shannon and Lanesborough.

The Board of Works, severely understaffed, was rapidly swamped with applications for relief projects. In many parts of the country, employment took months to begin. The demand for work massively exceeded available employment, and as the people, including women and children in some areas, flocked to the road works, farm labour was neglected. Wages were to be at most 12 to 13 pence per day. Although designed to attract commercial supplies of food, local traders were selling provisions at exorbitant prices well beyond what those employed on the works could afford. In 1846, subsistence for an average family would have cost approximately 2 to 3 shillings per day. Many did not receive employment even when recommended by the committees, and labourers were continually laid off so that the works would not be completed too soon. The workers' growing discontent led to a breakdown in relations between the Board of Works officials and the Relief Commissioners. A memo from Strokestown to the Commissioners reported on the 'refractory and ungrateful attitude' of some of Mahon's tenants employed on the works.

By June, it was apparent that purchase orders for more American grain could not be met because of prior orders from other European countries with grain shortages of their own. Largely because of his repeal of the Corn Laws, Peel's Tory government collapsed and was replaced by the Whigs under Lord John Russell. The new government resolved that the public works scheme had been a waste of money. A Treasury minute directed the closure of all public works in Ireland, except in cases of extreme need, by 8 August. Following a deluge of protest from the local Relief Committees, especially after the failure of the potato crop, the closing date was suspended.

With their commitment to the theories of political economy, which prioritised the almost sacred 'rights of Free Trade', the Whig government resolved to avoid emergency interventions in the market. Imports of grain or handouts of food were to be stopped and corn depots with remaining supplies were to be closed. In January 1847, Russell introduced an act for the provision of 'outdoor relief' – relief funded by local ratepayers, like the union workhouses, but provided outside the workhouses and with some Government aid. The act sought to encourage people to return to farm work by bringing the relief works to an end and opening soup kitchens throughout the country. By July 1847, the soup kitchens were providing three million people every day with cheap if not very nutritious food.

'...the Commissary General may entertain some refined notions of the rights of commerce... but I hope he will excuse me for telling him, there are some notions very good in Theory which would be very bad in Practice and the more so when a calamity like the present has disorganised the social relations of this country. The rights of Free Trade ought to be protected but O in the name of mercy and humanity extend them not to the present Free Traders in this country – give honest enterprise its due reward but let not the cupidity of the little Free Trader thrive on the Starvation of his kind – he excels in the penury and misery that surround him as Vultures do in the gasping writhings of their prey.'

Letter from Ballintober North Relief Committee, 26 March 1847.

In June, the Irish Poor Law Extension Act was passed, according to which there was to be no further Government aid for any form of relief in Ireland. Local rate-payers were now made entirely responsible for relieving destitution in their areas. Although many landowners had been unable to pay the old Poor Rate, they were now obliged to bear the expense of maintaining the poor outside the workhouses. Poor Rate rose as high as 50 per cent in Unions such as Westport, County Mayo. This act was the final ruin of many Irish landlords.

Private organisations attempted to compensate for the shortcomings of government aid. Conditions in Ireland had been widely reported by 1847, and significant relief was raised throughout the world. About £1 million was spent on famine relief by private charities, a considerable amount when set against the total £8 million spent by the government between 1845 and 1849. The British Association was set up by Stephen Spring Rice, son of the Limerick landlord Lord Monteagle, together with some of the richest merchants and industrialists in Britain. By 1850, the Association had raised £470,000, including a £2,000 donation from Queen Victoria. Grants were given to relief committees for food, clothing and fuel.

The Central Relief Committee of the Society of Friends "Quakers" was set up in Dublin and London in November 1846. The organisation commanded a vast network of fellow Quakers throughout Britain, Ireland and the United States, and by the time they closed operations in 1849 they had raised £200,000, one-half contributed by United States citizens. As well as distributing food, clothing and crop seeds, the Quakers sought to encourage industry and improve agriculture. They developed fishing stations at Achill, Ballinakill, Belmullet and Castletown Berehaven, and helped fishermen from other regions to redeem fishing gear which had been pawned or sold during periods of bad weather or outside the fishing season.

The Quakers closed their relief operations in 1849, declaring that charitable work was ultimately useless and could achieve no permanent benefit. This could happen only, they stated, through substantial reforms in laws relating to the sale or transfer of landed property, much of which, they pointed out, was heavily encumbered by debt or in the hands of middlemen. 'Our permanent want is not money', a Quaker circular from 1849 stated; 'it is the removal of those legal difficulties which prevent the capital of Ireland from being applied to the improved cultivation of its soil, and thus supporting its poor by the wages of honest and useful labour.'

During the bitter winter of 1846-47, members of the Quaker Relief Association made their way into the remoter districts of Munster and Connacht, to Schull and Skibbereen, County Cork, and to Erris and Belmullet, County Mayo. A few concerned private citizens also found themselves there, and a couple of correspondents for journals such as *The Illustrated London News*. Stunned, and in near disbelief, they tried to describe what they saw, claiming inability to convey the impact of the experience. These areas were beyond the reach of organised relief, but they were not, it was noted, devoid of food. The few doctors and clergymen active among the poor were unable to cope with the multitudes of sick and dying.

'On entering another house the doctor said, "Look there, Sir, you can't tell whether they are boys or girls". Taking up a skeleton child, he said: "Here is the way it is with them all; their legs swing and rock like the legs of a doll", and I saw that it was so in this instance. "Sir, they have the smell of mice." After I had seen a great number of these miserable objects, the doctor said, "Now, Sir, there is not a child you saw can live for a month; every one of them are in famine fever, a fever so sticky that it never leaves them..."'

'In none of the districts where I was did the case appear to me to be desperate; there was no want of food in any place... nor want of medicine, but there was the most deplorable want of available agency, and a consequent want of suitable measures to bring the food and the medicine within the reach of the people.'

Letter of F F Trench, curate of Cloghjordan, County Tipperary, 22 March 1847.

Eye-witnesses reported corpses lying unburied in the streets for days, sometimes gnawed by dogs and rats. Whole families were found dead inside cabins, children abandoned by their parents, and cases were documented of people eating dead and decaying livestock, even human flesh. Press reports of such circumstances shocked the public, and emergency collections for west Cork and other districts were well supported. In the early months of 1847, mortality began to rise as a result of epidemic diseases now raging through the country. Slowly, and despite withholding of funds by the government, Ireland's welfare system began to expand in an effort to cope with the crisis.

Although one of the poorest regions of Europe, Ireland maintained what one historian has called 'one of the most advanced health services in Europe', and supported a flourishing class of doctors, surgeons, apothecaries and other medical professionals. With only half the population of Liverpool, Dublin had more than twice the number of hospitals and almost double the amount of hospital beds. Unlike corresponding institutions in Britain, Dublin's hospitals received extensive funding from the British Treasury. Thirty seven infirmaries throughout the country were funded jointly by local government and the Central Board of Health. In addition, local subscribers maintained 70 fever hospitals for the segregation of patients with infectious diseases. Four hundred and fifty four regional communities, such as Strokestown, had their own dispensaries – medical supply centres – from which doctors ministered to the sick in the area.

A court for King Cholera, *Punch*

Connacht was the region least well provided with medical services, largely through the apathy or non-residence of potential subscribers. The barony of Frenchpark, County Roscommon, an area of 135 square miles (350 sq. ha) with a population of 30,000, had no hospital of any kind. In Mayo by 1845, there was one fever hospital and one infirmary for the county's 366,328 inhabitants. The Famine brought about further extension and improvement in the health system, principally with the opening of additional hospital accommodation through the Poor Law Commission, and with attempts to improve standards of hygiene by the Board of Health.

On 24 March 1846, the government passed a Temporary Fever Act. The act provided for the appointment of five commissioners to employ local medical officers and direct workhouse guardians to set up temporary fever hospitals and dispensaries where necessary. Despite warnings of an impending catastrophe, the commissioners decided by 31 August that fever statistics showed no cause for alarm, and the act was allowed to lapse. Nothing further was done for six months, until disturbing reports of death by thousands led to the appointment of a new Board of Health in February 1847.

The Board of Health had some success in forcing uncooperative workhouse guardians to provide fever accommodation in sheds adjacent to workhouses. In some areas, the Board sought to improve standards of hygiene by ventilating and whitewashing houses and by washing and disinfecting the inhabitants' clothes. It also provided funds to Relief Committees for the care of the sick in sheds and tents. The numbers treated in such temporary shelters from July 1847 to August 1850 amounted to over half a million, with mortality between 10 and 30 per cent. Doctors, nurses and voluntary workers attending the sick frequently fell victim to disease, chiefly typhus – the *rickettsia* which cause it are easily spread through the invisible means of louse excrement, which dries to a fine dust. One in every 13 medical officers died of epidemic diseases between 1846 and 1851; 191 medical personnel died in 1847 alone.

The existence of an 'advanced' health care system could not prevent massive mortality from treatable diseases, nor could it have done so with twice the resources. Like the Poor Law, the Board of Health was not designed to deal with the social and environmental causes of a crisis, but to contain its effects. Public spending on health was seen as a safeguard against the contamination of the more privileged classes. 'Expenses incurred for the cure of destitute fever patients may be regarded to a certain extent as a kind of life insurance for the rich who are in health', stated a circular letter to the Poor Law Unions on 6 October 1847. Furthermore, Dublin's famous research and teaching hospitals enabled the creation of high wage-earning professionals who found abundant research material in Dublin's extensive urban poor.

Although the Famine greatly magnified their effects, diseases such as the louse-borne fevers – typhus and relapsing fever – and dysentery were constantly prevalent in Ireland. The role of lice in the spread of fevers was not then understood. Typhus and relapsing fever were believed to be spread by 'exhalations' from the sick, while 'intemperance' was thought to be a predisposing factor. In 1851, the total reported figure for deaths from fever, without distinguishing between different types, was 192,937. The transmission of dysentery by a particular *bacillus* via hands, food or drinking water, was not then understood. It was believed to be caused by 'long continued exposure to high temperatures' and consumption of 'spirituous liquors'. Dysentery sufferers require rehydration, but the medical authorities of the time prescribed laxatives, blood-letting with leeches, and more solids in the diet. By 1851, the statistic for dysentery deaths – which probably also included other diseases such as infant diarrhoea – was 125,148. An epidemic of cholera raging throughout Europe in 1848 spread to Ireland and caused another 32,658 deaths (1851 census).

Eye-witnesses were often at pains to distinguish fever victims and those who died from 'actual starvation'. The 1851 census recorded 42,000 deaths from 'famine dropsy', a swelling of the limbs and organs due to malnutrition, although probably also symptomatic of other conditions such as typhus. Cases of the vitamin C deficiency-related illness known as scurvy or blackleg, previously rare in Ireland, were also reported.

The situation in the workhouse at Castlerea, County Roscommon is characteristic of the extreme strain under which the Poor Law Union system was operating in 1847. The Castlerea Union was in great debt, with 250 surplus inmates – it was built to accommodate 1,000 – by March 1847. There was no adequate drinking-water supply, and the staff could not cope with the filth of the buildings, even when inmates were paid to help them. Nobody could be found to remove the foul bedding and clothing from the yards. Excrement was taken away in barrows, but since the Union could not afford pitchforks, 'paupers' assigned to this duty had to load the barrows with their hands. There was no room for the isolation of the sick, and inmates fearful of infection refused to assist in carrying corpses to the limepits behind the house. On 3 April, of the total 1,115 inmates, 540 were sick with dysentery and 254 with typhus or relapsing fever. Deaths in March were as high as 74 per week. By late April, the doctor had resigned, the master and mistress of the house had died, and 830 of the 990 inmates had fever.

Land clearance and emigration: dispossession and exile

Scalpín of Pat O'Conor, Kilrush, County Clare

The pressures of an expanding population – overcrowding and the competition for land – had led to a constant stream of emigrants from Ireland during the late eighteenth and early nineteenth century. Emigration increased when the end of the Napoleonic Wars brought economic crisis and food shortages throughout Europe. One and a half million people left Ireland for North America between 1815 and 1845, amounting to one-third of the total trans-Atlantic emigrant traffic in these years. The emigrants tended to be mainly farmers and tradesmen of modest means. The cost of the passage exceeded the annual income of a rundale farmer or labourer.

Between 1845 and 1850 another one and a half million emigrated – almost one-fifth of Ireland's pre-Famine population. This chaotic, panic-stricken and unregulated exodus was the largest single population movement of the nineteenth century. In the year 1847 alone, 230,000 sailed to North America and Australia. Passenger Acts were passed to improve health and sanitary conditions on emigrant ships, but despite these measures 40,000 died at sea or in Canadian quarantine stations.

Emigration had been seen as a solution to Ireland's chief social problem – too many poor. Some members of Parliament proposed transplanting the populations of certain areas to Canada and recolonising the land with Protestant tenants. It was believed that Protestants would be more industrious and more cooperative with their landlord. Yet there was little government intervention, even after the scandals of 1847 reached Parliamentary debate.

The Poor Law Extension Act, which made landlords responsible for the maintenance of their own poor, induced some to clear their estates by paying for the emigration of their poorer tenants. Although some landlords claimed necessity and humanitarian motives, there were undoubted benefits to them, especially for those who wanted to redivide their land into larger holdings or to change from tillage to beef and dairy farming. Denis Mahon's agent, John Ross Mahon (1814-87), pointed out that it was ultimately cheaper than

The Peru leaving Cork for Melbourne

evicting tenants and paying rates for their maintenance in workhouses. He calculated that workhouse maintenance would cost £7 3s. per person for successive years, while the passage to Quebec would be less than half this annual amount. Faced with the prospect of the workhouse, tenants were, in general, willing to emigrate.

Emigration took a massive toll in the Strokestown area. In the diocese of Elphin, between one-tenth and one-fifth of the population of certain parishes left for North America in the first half of 1847. Among these were many parishes on the Mahon estate. Denis Mahon's agent sought to convince him that 'emigration on an extensive scale' was the only means of bringing his estate to order. According to the agent, the average quantity of land for every five people – the agent took this as the average family unit – was slightly more than four acres. Following the crop failures of 1845 and

1846, he surmised that the potato would have to be replaced by oats as the staple food of the tenant population. However, oats require a greater acreage, and the average family would need a holding of 12 acres (5 ha) in order to produce a year's crop. Two-thirds of the population, according to this calculation, would have to be cleared from the estate.

The agent's threat of resignation – because of the Major's reluctance to implement his recommendations – and the Poor Law

Emigration vessel, between decks, *Illustrated London News*

Extension Act of March 1847 finally persuaded Mahon to provide £4,000 for the passage and provisioning of more than 1,000 Strokestown tenants. Recent laws reducing the number of passengers per tonnage of ships had increased the cost of passage to the United States, and so it was decided to send the emigrants on the less expensive passage to Canada. Requests for passage began pouring in, but too many of the 'better class' of tenants were applying. 'I think', wrote Denis Mahon to his agent, 'the first class for us to send is those of the poorest and worst description, who would be a charge on us for the Poor House or for Outdoor Relief, and that would relieve the industrious tenant.' A charter was negotiated with a shipping firm in Liverpool, and Mahon instructed the agent to inspect the emigrants for fever. Such medical inspections were rushed and cursory at best, and the conditions in which the emigrants travelled, sometimes confined in bunks in the 'tween decks for weeks at a time, were squalid and unsanitary.

Tenants were sometimes given a small compensation (£5-£12) for their crops and livestock. Some who wanted to travel independently to the United States were given money towards the fare. Emigrants were given a sea-store consisting of tea, coffee, sugar, rice, oatmeal, dried fish and vinegar. 476 people boarded the *Virginius* at Liverpool, which set sail on 27 May; another 100 boarded the *Erin's Queen*. 350^{1}/2 adults – two children counted as one adult – sailed on the *Naomi* and fifty-five more on the *John Munn*.

On 4 August, *The Toronto Globe* reported on the arrival of the *Virginius*: 'The Virginius from Liverpool, with 496 passengers, had lost 158 by death, nearly one-third of the whole, and she had 180 sick; above one-half the whole will never see their home in the New World'. A medical officer at the quarantine station on Grosse Ile off Quebec reported that 'the few who were able to come on deck were ghastly, yellow-looking spectres, unshaven and hollow-cheeked... not more than six or eight were really healthy and able to exert themselves'. The crew of the ship were all ill, and seven had died. On the *Erin's Queen* 78 passengers had died and 104 were sick: 'the filth and dirt in this vessel's hold creates such an effluvium as to make it difficult to breathe'. On this ship the captain had to bribe the seamen with a sovereign for each body brought out from the hold. The dead sometimes had to be dragged out with boat hooks, since even their own relatives refused to touch them.

It has been calculated that five and a half thousand Irish emigrants died on Grosse Ile that summer. Those who made it to the mainland started an epidemic of dysentery and typhus which ravaged the cities of Quebec and Montreal. Canadian emigration officers wrote angry letters to the Colonial Secretary, Earl Grey, denouncing Irish landlords for brutally clearing their estates and dumping their pauperised tenantry on the colonies. The reports mentioned the Sligo tenants of Robert Gore-Booth and Lord Palmerston, those from the King's County estate of Lord de Vesci and those sent by Major Mahon.

Assisted emigration was a relatively humane form of clearance, and an option not available to many tenants dispossessed during and after the Famine. The clearance of conacre labourers, cottiers and rundale farmers had been contemplated by landlords and their agents before the onset of blight in 1845. By the 1840s, the main forms of obstruction to clearance had been weakened. Many middlemen had accumulated huge rent arrears and were evicted from their holdings along with their undertenants. John Ross Mahon's survey of eight townlands on the estate, an area of 2,105 acres (851 ha), recorded 479 families (2,444 persons), most of whom had not paid any rent in two years. Popular organisations, which had forcibly resisted attempts to terminate conacre or to enclose land for grazing, were weakened by starvation and disease. The areas of the country where evictions predominantly took place during the Famine – Tipperary, Limerick, Clare, Leitrim and Roscommon – had previously been noted for the activities of secret societies. The Poor Law system also facilitated clearance, since tenants could not qualify for admission to the workhouses if they maintained holdings of more than one-quarter of an acre.

When a tenant fell into arrears, a warrant to distrain was issued by the sheriff and cattle, crops and other property was seized. A Bill of Ejectment then compelled the tenant to surrender his or her holding and cabin. Frequently, tenants were turned out by force, with the help of the militia and the house was often demolished to prevent its re-occupation. Sometimes, labourers on public works projects returned in the evenings to find their cabins pulled down in their absence.

'…property would be valueless and capital would no longer be invested in cultivation of land if it were not acknowledged that it was the landlord's undoubted, indefeasible and most sacred right to deal with his property as he list.'

Lord Brougham, House of Lords, 23 March 1846.

In 1846, a total of 4,599 actions for ejectment were brought in urban and rural properties. In 1849, 16,686 families were evicted, 19,949 the following year. In 1847, slightly more than 3,000 tenants were evicted at Strokestown; this was higher than the estimated total for County Cork – 2,436 – for that year. Strokestown was one of several estates where plans were made to colonise the cleared land with Protestant tenants, but there appears to have been little or no response to advertisements placed in the Scottish newspapers by Mahon's agent in 1848.

A token compensation was occasionally given to the evicted tenants – a small amount of money, a forgiving of arrears, sometimes the right to keep crops and livestock. A form of compensation frequently granted in Cork was the right to keep the thatch and timbers of the destroyed cabin, with which the dispossessed family could then construct a temporary shelter in a ditch or on waste ground, known as a *scailpín*. Others resorted to holes in banks of earth, roofed with sods and branches, known as a *scailp*. If these were erected on the landlord's property the evicted families were hunted out by bailiffs.

On 7 November 1848, a poor law commissioner reported from Kilrush, County Clare, that the evicted were 'swarming all over the Union, living in temporary sheds unfit for human occupation, from which they are daily driven by the inclement weather'. He described scalps constructed in ditches with branches and sods of earth, turf and furze. Nearly 7,000 were evicted in Kilrush between August 1848 and January 1849. Images of evicted people in the Kilrush Union were published in *The Illustrated London*

News in 1848. They sought to raise public sympathy by showing the homeless as passive, dazed and helpless. This may, however, have had the negative effect of reinforcing the existing stereotypes of the Irish poor as complacent in their misery and incapable of improvement, a note sounded in the following account of an eviction from December 1849: 'Nothing could exceed the heartlessness of the levellers, if it were not the patient submission of the sufferers. They wept, indeed, and the children screamed with agony at seeing their houses destroyed and their parents in tears: but the latter allowed themselves unresistingly to be deprived of what is to most people the dearest thing earth next to their lives – their only homes.'

Driving cattle for rent between Ouchterard and Galway, *Illustrated London News*

In December 1846, John Ross Mahon began to serve eviction notices against tenants who were in arrears with their rent. Some petitioned the Major, requesting that they be left in their homes at least for the remainder of the winter. The Major believed that most of these were troublemakers 'who are known to be able to pay and only refuse from combination. These tenants I should be glad to get rid of on any terms'. A 'combination' was an organised resistance to the payment of rent and it had been pioneered locally by tenants on the Crown estate of Ballykilcline, Kilglass, County Roscommon. On certain townlands the Major hoped that, under threat of eviction, some of the rent arrears could be recovered thereby forestalling further ejectments, 'altho' I am aware the law admits of my taking possession, yet I would willingly, in the present state of the people, make any sacrifice sooner than put the law in force'. Yet his plan of redividing and redistributing the land on some portions of the estate was resisted by the tenants. In exasperation, Mahon insisted that no toleration be shown to those who objected: 'I shall have notice served on them all, I shall evict the whole, and not one of them shall get the land again'.

'The court of the black sheep office'

Right boys paying their tythes

'A better treatment of the poor in Ireland is a very material point to the welfare of the whole British Empire. Events may happen which may convince us fatally of this truth – if not, oppression must have broken all the spirit and resentment of men. By what policy the government of England can for so many years have permitted such an absurd system to be matured in Ireland, is beyond the power of plain sense to discover.'

Arthur Young, *A Tour in Ireland*, 1770

The Strokestown rent-strike, which, according to the agent had been in existence before the first potato failure in 1845, was part of a marked increase throughout the country of militant activity by secret societies of tenants and labourers against landlords and farmers. Described in 1836 as 'vast trade unions for the protection of Irish peasantry', such groups had their origins in agrarian movements of the eighteenth century, when under the Penal Laws both Catholics and Presbyterians were deprived of the legal rights enjoyed by the Church of Ireland ruling classes. Oakboys had organised in protest at enforced labour on the roads in Ulster, while Rightboys attacked collectors of tithes – compulsory dues for the maintenance of Church of Ireland clergy. Some groups, such as the Caravats and the Shanavests in early nineteenth century Munster and south Leinster, represented the factional struggles of labourers and strong farmers. Factionalism sometimes had a sectarian character: the Protestant Peep O'Day Boys fought the Catholic Defenders in 1790s Armagh, and Rockites in the 1820s were dedicated to a rising against 'English heretics'.

Members of secret societies took oaths, frequently operated by night or during the day disguised as women (known as Lady Rocks). Although their oaths professed allegiance to the Pope, Ribbonmen struck at Catholic strong farmers, magistrates, Poor Rate collectors and against fellow tenants who refused to take their oath of membership or who occupied the holdings of evicted tenants. In 1820, the police at Castlerea, County Roscommon alerted Dublin Castle that an entire army of Ribbonmen was preparing to attack the town. By the 1830s, a more common strategy was the organising of strikes or 'combinations' against the payment of rent, especially on the badly run and bankrupt estates of the west of Ireland.

During the famine years, assassinations of land owners increased leading to the demand for stronger government action against secret societies. Coercion laws were passed which made 'agrarian outrage' punishable by transportation or by the death penalty. Landlords, politicians and the anti-Irish press in Britain saw these activities as instigated by the critics of British policy in Ireland – Daniel O'Connell's association for the repeal of the Act of Union, the Young Ireland movement and members of the Catholic clergy.

The Roman Catholic Irish bishops were represented in *The Times* as architects of a great sectarian conspiracy to eliminate Protestant landlords and clergymen. The Catholic clergy had become increasingly active in politics after the repeal of the last anti-Catholic laws in 1829. Some spoke out against the injustices of British rule in Ireland and the abuses of the landlord system. While there appears to have been a genuine concern for social reform, this activity was also to some extent motivated by a desire to further the power and authority of the church. The principal clashes between clergy and government occurred over issues such as the establishment of non-denominational state-supported schools. Most clergy preached conformity with law and order and condemned secret societies.

During the Famine, Catholic priests served alongside Protestant clergymen on Relief Committees and exerted themselves to feed and alleviate the plight of the suffering poor. Many lost their own means of support as their parishioners died or emigrated. Some were reported to have preached sermons against landlords, hinting to their congregations that they should take justice into their own hands. The government demanded that the hierarchy discipline militant tendencies within the clergy, but Bishop McHale of Tuam, County Galway, and Bishop Browne of Elphin, County Roscommon responded by defending them. In 1848, a propaganda war followed between these bishops and the conservative press.

Although diplomatic links between England and the Vatican are forbidden under British law, the Government sent a delegation to Rome in early 1848. The mission was partly the result of efforts by Lord Shrewsbury, a zealous Catholic peer who sought to establish diplomatic relations between Britain and Rome, which he believed to be jeopardised by the threat of rebellion in Ireland. On 5 February 1848, the Irish bishops received a Papal Rescript demanding that the clergy refute the charges of inciting rebellion levelled against them. The Papal intervention had the effect of silencing more outspoken members of the clergy.

The 1840s, throughout Europe, was a decade of mounting challenge to the aristocratic regimes restored to power after the Napoleonic Wars. The Republican visions and idealism of the period were sometimes aligned with programmes of real social reform. Although often portrayed as misguided romantics, the group known as Young Ireland attempted to provide a form of leadership directly connected to the concerns of the people. The movement was born from a split in the ranks of the Repeal Association following Daniel O'Connell's renunciation of armed struggle as a means of gaining independence for Ireland. Most of the breakaway group were associated with *The Nation* newspaper: the name imitated that of a continental republican movement, Mazzini's Young Italy. Some of the leaders espoused a vision of a union of all classes, Catholics and Protestants, against England. Others wanted instant revolution, or advocated a general rent strike of all the country's tenant farmers.

'Matters look very threatening in Roscommon', wrote Denis Kelly, a relative of Major Mahon, to The O'Conor Don in late August 1846; 'last week a large assembly paraded near Castlerea with a loaf on a pole and a placard FOOD OR BLOOD, and there was a similar assemblage at Loughrea. There was to have been one here at Castle Kelly but I was able to prevent it by my private influence. Two troops of dragoons are ordered to Roscommon and the executive are quite alive to the danger.' Denis Mahon was informed a few weeks later that certain persons were collecting money 'for attorney O'Farrell to give your honour opposition and obstruction in collecting your rent and arrears'. When the writer declined to contribute he was menaced by 'Night Men' and received warning that if he paid his rent he would be 'burned alive'. A petition of 22 August to Mahon from the men of Cloonahee, who had been dismissed from the public works, promised violent action as the only alternative if they were not provided with food and work:

'Our families are well and truly suffering in our presence and we cannot much longer withstand their cries for food. We have no food for them, our potatoes are rotten and we have no grain... And, Gentlemen, you know but little of the state of the suffering poor... Are we to resort to outrage? Gentlemen, we fear that the peace of the country will be much disturbed if relief be not more extensively afforded to the suffering peasantry. We are not for joining in anything illegal or contrary to the laws of God or the land unless pressed to by HUNGER.'

Besides the climate of fear and antagonism between landlord and tenants, there was open hostility between Mahon and the local Catholic clergy. In July 1846, he had attacked the priests for 'feasting and stuffing and praying here these last weeks' while their flocks were starving. In September, three priests complained to the Relief Commission of the 'undisguised bigotry' of Mahon, who had appointed only two Catholics to the seven-member Relief Committee in Strokestown.

Having spent a few months in England, during which time the agent had arranged the assisted emigration of more than 800 tenants to Canada, Denis Mahon attended a meeting of the Strokestown Relief

Committee on 28 August 1847. Fr Michael McDermott, parish priest of Strokestown, had acted as chairman in his absence. At the meeting Mahon queried the accounts and the lists of persons entitled to relief. According to Mahon's own account, which was read in the House of Lords after his death,

'Fr Mc Dermott rose up in a violent passion and asked how I dared to come there and terrorise over him? How dare I come at the eleventh hour, after leaving him to do all the work, and attack him by my "side wind" allusions, but that he would not bear it; he had a hand to defend himself, and would do so. He was certainly in a violent passion, and would not listen to my repeated assurances that I had not in the slightest manner said, or intended to say, anything to annoy him... However, all I could say was of no use; he still continued to repeat that I had come, when all the business had been done by him, to find fault and tyrannise over him; that I spent my winter in London to amuse myself, and had left my people to starve in the streets and die, without ever looking after them; that I had done nothing for them, and had no right now to come and interfere, and also he stated to me that I had not done anything for the poor since my return, but had amused myself burning houses and turning out the people to starve. That, I was obliged to assure the reverend gentleman, was not the case, and that whatever I did with regard to my property I conceived rested with myself, and that I would not allow him or any man to meddle with me in that respect, and desired him not to presume to meddle in my private affairs.'

Two months later, on 2 November, Mahon attended a further meeting of the Board of Guardians at Roscommon Union workhouse. On his return that evening, he passed Four Mile House in the townland of Doorty. As he crossed Doorty bridge an unseen marksman fired two shots, the second of which struck Mahon in the chest, killing him instantly.

Major Denis Mahon

A general panic broke out in the area. A new Coercion Act was passed and large numbers of police and military were quartered in Strokestown House and its neighbourhood. 'This county', reported the *Dublin Evening Mail,* 'is like a scene of open rebellion'. On 6 November, *The Times* reported that the event had adversely affected property values and estates offered for sale could not be sold. The assassination of the Major was immediately followed by threats to other Roscommon landlords and attempts were made on the lives of Lord Crofton of Mote Park, Denis Kelly of Castle Kelly, and William Talbot of Mount Talbot. With the murder of the Reverend John Lloyd of Croghan some weeks later, rumours became rife of an extensive conspiracy for exterminating Protestant landlords, and of a 'satanic conclave' in the diocesan seat of Elphin. It was reported that Fr McDermott had denounced Major Mahon from the pulpit the Sunday before the assassination, saying 'Major Mahon is worse than Cromwell, and yet he lives'.

Lord Shrewsbury led the call for disciplinary action against McDermott, and detectives attended masses throughout the country to record any other denunciations from the altar. In the House of Commons Irish Liberal members of Parliament blamed the murder on Mahon's emigration scheme, citing a false rumour that one of the ships had sunk: 'Nothing could persuade the people' said Henry Grattan Junior on 23 November 'that emigration was not a plot against their lives. Added to this, it was stated that Major Mahon said he would make a sheepwalk of Strokestown.' In a public reply to Shrewsbury printed in *The Freeman's Journal*, 29 April 1848, Bishop George Browne of Elphin declared he could find no evidence against the parish priest. He published a list of 3,006 tenants dispossessed by Mahon's agent, most of whom, he said, were now dead.

The motives for Mahon's murder do not appear to have been sectarian, nor can it be seen as a spontaneous act in revenge for emigration or eviction. It appears that it was a result of a conspiracy which targeted landlords as enemies of the people and which was confident of popular support. Whatever the motive, the people claimed the murder as a victory for themselves – it was reported that they had lit bonfires throughout the area in celebration – even though they were soon to suffer as a result of the act. Militant tenant organisations cited the murder in menacing letters to landlords, threatening them with the 'fate of Major Mahon'. The murder was politically exploited at a higher level: the nationalist and pro-repeal press, while deploring the murder, cited it as a consequence of the evils of the landlord system and of English misrule. Conservatives demanded repressive measures against the people and the Catholic church. Aid to Ireland, they claimed, was being spent on guns and not food. The Whig government kept a characteristic distance, regarding agrarian violence as an internal Irish problem for which the country's feckless landlords were to blame. 'It is quite true that landlords in England would not like to be shot like hares or partridges', said Lord John Russell, 'but neither does any landlord in England turn out fifty persons at once and burn their houses over their heads, giving them no provision for the future.'

However, fear of a more general and systematic rebellion in Ireland increased steadily. Throughout 1848 a series of armed uprisings in Paris, Budapest, Berlin and other cities convulsed the established order across Europe, and Young Ireland was inspired to plan an armed revolution of its own. Rather than organising and recruiting secretly, they called for revolution in the columns of *The Nation* and expected the people to rally when the cry was raised. The government struck first: under special emergency legislation the entire country was garrisoned with police and military. This was not only in anticipation of an organised rising, but because of the general collapse in public order. Commercial transports of food from the countryside to the ports were granted armed protection. Most of the Young Ireland leaders were arrested. William Smith O'Brien (1803-64), who had tried unsuccessfully to rally the people of north Munster, was captured with a small band of followers after a skirmish at Ballinagarry, County Tipperary. The leaders were deported to Tasmania. Smith O'Brien returned as editor of *The Nation* in 1856. His Young Ireland associates Thomas Francis Meagher (1823-67) and John Mitchell (1815-75) later pursued successful journalistic and political careers in the United States and continued to publicise their version of the nationalist cause.

The Famine was not the sole reason for Young Ireland's lack of success, but the rising had significant consequences for the popular memory of the Famine, especially for emigrants. Writers such as Mitchell and Meagher encouraged people to see their sufferings in political – ultimately in nationalist – terms, as the result of domination by a foreign power. They also reinvigorated the Republican dream of 1798 for a generation of Irish emigrants and their descendants.

Denis Mahon's son-in-law and successor, Henry Sandford Pakenham Mahon, ordered the immediate eviction of tenants in the area where the Major was shot. The tenants sent petitions to the agent, assuring him that they had paid their rents regularly until the failure of the potato crop. They begged to be allowed remain in their holdings and protested their innocence of the murder of Major Mahon: 'they beseech for the

Lord's sake that the act of such savage wretches will not be the means of casting them and their large families to perish houseless by the ditchside in a cold and severe winter.' In forwarding this petition to Pakenham Mahon, the agent wrote 'would you approve of the tenants who are anxious to stay being informed that they will be allowed to do so if the murderers are surrendered? I do not think it would have any effect but it is possible that it might'. At least one tenant, a farmer's son named James Hunt, gave information and fled to Manchester to avoid being used as a witness in court. Three men from the area had been arrested by late February: Patrick Hasty, the keeper of a *shebeen* (premises selling illicit spirits), James Cummins, a 'dead shot', and Patrick Doyle, a labourer. Among the key witnesses were John Hestor, a servant of Hasty dismissed for 'stealing turnips', and an army pensioner named James Rigney whom the conspirators had tried to recruit as an assassin. The witnesses, often including their entire families, were detained, in the overcrowded, unsanitary conditions of Roscommon gaol, where one of the chief witnesses died from fever after reportedly confessing the innocence of all the parties he had named.

The trial took place at the assizes on 12 July, with the Attorney General as Counsel for the Prosecution. The charge for conspiracy was considered by him to be be stronger than that for the actual murder. The witnesses, described as 'bad characters', were hooted by the crowd on the day of the trials. Among them was James Donnelly, who told of 'a great consultation to know whether it was Major Mahon or Sir Ross Mahon, the agent, they should shoot'. Hasty was found guilty of conspiring to murder Denis Mahon. 'You have not even a pretence of grievance respecting yourself' said the judge, Baron Lefroy, ' ...that could account for you entering into a conspiracy.' Hasty protested his innocence and asserted that he had no object or benefit in the murder of the Major. He also pointed out that he was not a tenant on the Strokestown estate and that he knew the Major to be a good landlord.

By nine o'clock the next day the jury had reached no verdict in the trial of Cummins. 'Baron Lefroy's charge to the Jury was strong against the prisoner', wrote Denis Mahon's brother to the Major's widow, 'but... two or three fellows on the jury were determined not to find him guilty.' By the next day, several members of the jury were ill with fever, and the remaining trials were postponed to the next assizes. Meanwhile, reports circulated of the success of Smith O'Brien campaign in the south and south-west of the country and of a vast network of revolutionary cells and spontaneous gatherings of 50,000 men wherever Smith O'Brien made an appearance.

The execution of Hasty took place on the 8 August, several days after the Young Ireland debacle in Ballingarry, County Tipperary. There were elaborate military preparations to forestall rioting or the prisoner's rescue: 'On Monday a squadron of Scotch Greys arrived here at about 12 o'clock from Athlone' reported *The Freeman's Journal*, 10 August, 'and in two hours after two companies of the 31st in addition to one stationed, marched in, together with upward of one hundred of the constabulary from the out stations.' Hasty's confession to conspiracy and 'knowledge and participation of that accursed system of Molly Maguireism' was printed and circulated by John Ross Mahon. 'There was a very large attendance at Hasty's funeral', wrote the agent on 12 August, 'which clearly shows the feeling of the people to be as bad as ever.'

The aftermath: 'a conspiracy of silence'

A strong farmer and his wife, 1870s

'I am happy to say that the *haberes* have been executed without any incident or disturbance. The levelling of the Houses has been done most effectively – there is not a wall left standing and the stones are removed to the foundation. There was no case of Fever or Sickness which I consider very fortunate. It was thought advisable by Mr Blakeney, the subinspector of Police that the houses belonging to Michael Gardiner who is now in Gaol and John McNamara both of Doorty should be left standing; it is possible that both persons may be of use in giving information.'

John Ross Mahon to Henry Sandford Pakenham Mahon, 3 August 1848.

'The fact is, society in Roscommon is completely disorganised and it will take years to reconstruct the social fabric there, particularly under the 'laissez aller' system of the Whigs, and under such circumstances my advice to you is to forget for five years at least that you have such a thing as property in Roscommon, to leave it totally in the hands of your agent. Amuse yourself and your dear wife as youth and circumstances will, for the present, and trust to a gracious Providence that at that time you will have a chance of returning to an altered country and breaking entirely fresh ground. I think that Galway will recover much sooner and that if peace can be preserved another year will see us much as usual here, but in Roscommon (particularly your part of it) I have no hopes of any real amendment for five years.'

Denis Kelly to Henry Sandford Pakenham Mahon, landlord of Strokestown, 11 June 1848.

Two hundred ejectments were served on the Strokestown estate in August 1848, at a time when it was increasingly evident that the potato crop would fail again. Pakenham Mahon demanded greater stringency in the payment of compensation to evicted tenants. He allowed the agent to distribute £200 'with great caution' among no less than two hundred evicted families. More petitions were received from the remaining tenants of Doorty and adjoining townlands. 'Possibly they are worthy of some consideration', wrote the agent, 'though it is scarcely probable that they were not in some measure privy to what was going on... There are one hundred families on the lands of Cornashina, Leitrim Castle and Doorty – and we have *haberes* against as many more on other townlands. I wish you to be in full possession of the facts as no doubt the Press will take up the subject.'

Strokestown had by that point become a byword for mass-eviction. The Catholic Bishop of Elphin was one of a number of influential individuals who had publicly attacked Irish landlords for their negligence, cruelty and ruthless efficiency in carrying out evictions. John Ross Mahon and Denis Mahon's heir responded with an attempt to embarrass the Bishop by publicising the fact that his own brother Patrick Browne, a middleman on the Strokestown estate, had himself carried out evictions of under-tenants on his holdings at Cloonfad. The Bishop's retaliated by publishing a list of 3,006 persons evicted in Mahon's name before the assassination, in *The Freeman's Journal*, 29 April 1848, accompanied by a leader entitled 'The Strokestown Massacre Developed'.

The agent nonetheless continued his policy of clearance – enforcing the payment of arrears, eliminating middlemen, encouraging and subsidising emigration. The huge volume of homelessness and poverty created by these policies was to some extent relieved by establishing the Strokestown area as a Union in its own right. Under pressure from the Poor Law Commissioners a workhouse was eventually constructed outside the town at Cloonslanor. It opened in 1852. This remained in service until 1920 when, under a scheme to reduce the number of workhouses in the area, the Strokestown Union was re-amalgamated with Roscommon. Nothing now remains of the Strokestown workhouse but 'bully's acre', a prehistoric earthwork which was used as a cemetery.

Roscommon cathedral, 1890s

The disappearance of the Strokestown workhouse was symptomatic of a general tendency to erase the physical traces of the Great Famine amongst survivors and their descendants. A century afterwards, very little folklore or storytelling about the great trauma survived. People were reluctant, even ashamed, to admit that there had been much suffering among their ancestors or in their part of the country. 'Indeed' wrote a reporter to the Irish Folklore Commission in 1945 'it seems there was a sort of conspiracy of silence on the part of their fathers and mothers about it all.'

Because the Famine resulted from social and political inequalities, and because its discussion raises highly emotive issues and ethical questions, the historical record itself has become highly contentious. For almost a century, the history of the Great Famine

Children, Garumna Island, whose father is on the relief works, 1895

was largely written by Irish nationalists. The Famine was regarded by John Mitchell, by The Fenians, by some Home Rulers, by Patrick Pearse and others as an official mass-murder, epitomising the intolerable nature of British rule in Ireland. Later historians, in pursuit of 'objectivity', saw such accounts as propaganda and tried to minimise the horrors of the Famine in their writings. However, a new consciousness of the Famine and its meaning in Irish history has arisen through the spectacle of worsening poverty, of millions of deaths still occurring throughout the world because of exploitation, indifference and the law of the free-market.

The Great Irish Famine was the greatest social catastrophe of nineteenth century Europe. It began a process of depopulation which transformed the rural landscape. The loss of two and an half million people through death and emigration decimated an entire class – the landless rural labourer. Emigration continued to reduce the population of Roscommon. Between 1851 and 1881 the population of the Strokestown area alone declined by a staggering 88 per cent, making it one of the worst affected areas in the country. Rundale and conacre farming largely disappeared and tillage farming was replaced by less labour-intensive cattle rearing on larger farm units. By 1854, livestock accounted for half of the total agricultural output. Between 1845 and 1851 one farm in four disappeared. Those that remained tended to be holdings of upwards of fifteen acres. Connacht was the slowest to change: small farms persisted and the potato remained the principal crop. The exception was on 'progressively' managed estates such as Strokestown, where small holdings were consolidated to make large grazing farms. Evicted tenants from Strokestown and central Roscommon moved to live to the bogs and wastelands of the north and west of the county, areas whose population had increased by 1851 and which were to be classified as 'congested districts' by the end of the century.

Although Poor Rates and arrears ruined many Irish landlords, the great estates of Roscommon survived the Famine intact. The preservation of Strokestown was largely enabled by its amalgamation, through the marriage of Denis Mahon's daughter, with the 20,000 acre property of the Sandford Pakenhams of Castlerea. In 1849, the Encumbered Estates court was set up to facilitate the sale of bankrupt properties, which in Roscommon were mainly those of the smaller landlords who held less than 1,000 acres.

The standard account of Irish society after the Great Famine runs along these lines: the transfer of bankrupt estates made possible the rise of the Irish middle class farmer and his dominance in rural society, along with shopkeepers and professionals. Their values and attitudes were imitated by the poorer classes. Family and social life became more anglicised and more regulated by the influence of the Catholic Church. The use of the Irish language diminished greatly. The scatterings of small villages or *clacháns* across the countryside disappeared and were replaced by the isolated two-storey farmhouse. The shift symbolises the replacement of the more communal 'extended family' of traditional peasant culture to the Catholic nuclear family of modern Ireland.

In the typical post-Famine family only the eldest son inherited the family farm. Daughters and younger sons had less access to land of their own on which they could support a family, hence they tended to marry less and later in life. Many emigrated, entered religious orders, or remained at home unmarried. Single women were one of the most prominent groups to emigrate from Ireland. Having greater access to education, the farmer and his family were more literate, and tended to speak English rather than Irish. Their religious observances were increasingly controlled by a centralised and authoritarian clergy. Weekly attendance at mass, the stations of the cross, the rosary, devotion to the Sacred Heart and the Immaculate Conception, represented the inroads of the new official Catholicism, which often sought to displace the old observance of patterns, wakes, faith healers, holy wells and bonfires. The grandiose post-famine churches which dominate many Irish towns are the most eloquent testimony to the arrival of a new class in Irish society.

This is one version of history. Its bleakness masks a loss of detail. Its linear and generalised approach conceals and effaces the great contrasts in Irish life after the Famine, the persistence and widening of local and regional differences, and the varying experiences of progress and stagnation at local levels. The experience of living in a modernising and prosperous Ireland was, and is still, affected by one of the major forces in Irish life since the Famine – the experience of living in the 'other Ireland' created by emigration, which has been crucial for the formation of collective and uniform notions of Irish identity. Now, 150 years after the Famine, emigration also provides the sense of contact with a broader global community, of a common identity and history with other groups and nationalities.

The opening of a museum devoted to the Great Famine is perhaps a sign of how a number of present experiences, national and global, return us to a consideration of the past. The national experiences include the huge economic importance of tourism and heritage and the ongoing depopulation of the country through emigration. The causal relation of these developments must be explained, rather than merely exploited, in the marketing of Irish history and heritage, a process which usually elides unpleasant facts or relegates them to a safe historical distance. The global experience is the exploitative relation of North and South, in which Ireland's growing participation is facilitated by the ongoing 'conspiracy of silence' about its own past. The neglect of the historical perspective afforded by events such as the Great Famine has led to the world's ability to tolerate the ongoing state of poverty and starvation in the developing world. As the voice of this developing world finds a response, Ireland can reconsider the meaning of its history.

Bibliographical notes

The following material was used in the preparation of the Famine Museum and of this publication:

Documentary sources
The Pakenham Mahon papers, Strokestown Park and the National Library of Ireland, Dublin; The O'Conor papers, Clonalis, Castlerea; Minutes of Castlerea Union workhouse, Roscommon County Library; Relief Commission papers, Public Records Office of Ireland (National Archives); State of the Country Papers and Crime and Outrage Papers (National Archives); Famine Survey by the Irish Folklore Commission, Department of Folklore, U.C.D.; Irish Architectural Archive.

Primary sources
Census of 1841 HC 1843 (504), xxiv; *Census of 1851* Part V, Vol. 1, Tables of deaths. HC 1856 (2087-1), xxix, 261; *Freeman's Journal*, Dublin; *Gardener's Chronicle*, London; J. O'Rourke, *A History of the Great Irish Famine* (Dublin, 1874); Pim, J., *The Condition and Prospects of Ireland* (Dublin, 1848);Poor Inquiry: Appendix D to the First Report of Inquiry into the Condition of the Poor in Ireland, HC 1836 (36), XXXI,1; Poor Inquiry: Appendix E to the First Report of Inquiry into the Condition of the Poor in Ireland, HC 1836 (37), xxxii, 1; *Roscommon Journal*, Roscommon; Smith, E., *Journals*. ed. D. Thomson and M. McGinty, *The Irish Journals of Elizabeth Smith 1840-1850* (Oxford, 1980); Trench, W. S., *Realities of Irish Life* (Dublin, 1868); Trevelyan, C., *The Irish Crisis* (London, 1848); Tuke, J. H. etc. *Transactions of the Central Relief Committee of the Society of Friends during the Famine in Ireland* (Dublin, 1852); Walford, C. 'The Famines of the World: Past and Present,' *Journal of the Royal Statistical Society*, xli 1878 pt. iii and xlii 1879;Weld, I. *Statistical Survey of the County of Roscommon* (Dublin, 1832); Whyte, R. *The Ocean Plague, or a Voyage to Quebec in an Irish Emigrant Vessel by 'A Cabin Passenger'* (London, 1848); Young, A. *A Tour in Ireland* (London, 1780).

Modern histories of the Great Famine
R. D. Edwards and T. D. Willams, *The Great Famine* (Dublin, 1957); C. Woodham-Smith, *The Great Hunger* (London, 1962); M. Daly, *The Famine in Ireland* (Dublin, 1986); C. Ó Gráda, *The Great Irish Famine* (London, 1989); E. M. Crawford, ed. *Famine. The Irish Experience* (Edinburgh, 1989). See also the chapters by J. S. Donnelly in W. E. Vaughan, ed. *A New History of Ireland V: Ireland Under the Union I, 1801-1870* (Oxford, 1989).

Ireland before the Union and ascendancy culture
E. M. Johnston, *Ireland in the Eighteenth Century* (Dublin, 1974); R. F. Foster, *Modern Ireland, 1600-1972* (London, 1988); L. P. Curtis 'Incumbered Wealth: Landed Indebtedness in Post-Famine Ireland,' *The American Historical Review* 85/2 (1980).

Rural economy and society
K. H. Connell, *The Population of Ireland, 1750-1845* (Oxford, 1951); P. J. Carty, *The Historical Geography of County Roscommon, with special reference to changes landownership settlement and population distribution*, M.A. thesis, National University of Ireland, 1970 (Carty's indispensable work is the source of the information included above on Lord de Freyne and his middlemen and on the population decline in the Strokestown area after the Famine); J. S. Donnelly, *The Land and People of Nineteenth Century Cork: The Rural Economy and the Land Question* (London, 1975); D. J. Casey and R. E. Rhodes, eds. *Views of the Irish Peasantry 1800-1916* (Hamden, CT 1977); Joel Mokyr, *Why Ireland Starved: A Quantitative and Analytical History of the Irish Economy, 1800-1850* (London, 1982); S. Clark and J. S. Donnelly, *Irish Peasants: Violence and Political Unrest 1780-1914* (Madison WN, 1983); M.J. Winstanley, *Ireland and the Land Question* (London, 1984); A. O'Dowd, *Spalpeens and Tattie Hokers: History and Folklore of the Irish Migratory Agricultural Worker in Ireland and Britain* (Dublin, 1991).

The potato in Ireland, diet, and the coming of blight
R. N. Salaman, *The History and Social Influence of the Potato* (Cambridge, 1949, 1985); E. C. Nelson, 'David Moore, Miles J. Berkeley and scientific studies of potato blight in Ireland, 1845-7,' *Archives of Natural History*, xi (1983); M. Crawford and L. A. Clarkson, 'Dietary Directions: A Topographical Survey of irish Diet, 1836' in R. Mitchison and P. Roebuck, eds. *Economy and Society in Scotland and Ireland 1500-1939* (Edinburgh, 1988); Austin Bourke (ed. J. Hill and C Ó'Gráda) '*The Visitation of God? The Potato and the Great Irish Famine* (Dublin, 1993).

Famine relief, medicine and mortality

H. Burke, *The People and the Poor Law in Nineteenth Century Ireland* (Dublin, 1987); O. MacDonagh, 'Public health: dispensaries and hospitals,' in *A New History of Ireland* (MacDonagh provides the phrase 'a golden age of Irish medicine'); Donnelly, 'Excess Mortality and Emigration,' ibid.

Emigration

T. Coleman, *A Passage to America* (London, 1972); M. O'Gallagher, *Grosse Ile: Gateway to Canada 1832-1937* (Quebec, 1984); K. A. Miller, *Emigrants and Exiles: Ireland and the Irish Exodus to North America* (Oxford, 1985); P. O'Farrell, *The Irish in Australia* (Kensington, New South Wales, 1986); R. Reid, 'Green Threads of Kinship: Irish Chain Migration to New South Wales, 1820-1886,' *Familia* 2/3 1987; R. Scally, 'Liverpool Ships and Irish Emigrants in the Age of Sail,' *Journal of Social History*, 17/1 1987; W. Donald Mackay, *Flight from Famine: The Coming of the Irish to Canada* (London and Toronto, 1990); J. O'Brien and P. Travers, eds. *The Irish Emigrant Experience in Australia* (Dublin, 1991).

'Agrarian Outrages'

T. D. Williams, ed. *Secret Societies in Ireland* (Dublin, 1973); J. S. Donnelly jr. 'Whiteboy Movements" *Irish Historical Studies* 21 (1978); J. Lee, 'Patterns of Rural Unrest in Nineteenth Century Ireland,' in L. Cullen and F. Furet, eds *Ireland and France, 17th-20th Centuries* (Ann Arbor, 1980); T. Garvin, 'Defenders, Ribbonmen and Others: Underground Political Networks in Pre-Famine Ireland,' *Past and Present* 96 (1982); M. R. Beames, *Peasants and Power: Whiteboy Movements and their Control in Pre-Famine Ireland* (New York, 1983).

After the Famine

J. J. Lee, *The Modernisation of Irish Society, 1848-1918* (Dublin, 1983); K. Whelan, 'The Famine and Post-Famine Adjustment,' in W. Nolan, ed. *The Shaping of Ireland: The Geographical Perspective* (Dublin, 1986); W. E. Vaughan, *Landlords and Tenants in Ireland, 1848-1904* (Dublin, 1984); V. A. Walsh, 'The Great Famine and its Consequences,' *Eire-Ireland* 23/4, 1988; Ó'Gráda, *Ireland Before and After the Famine* (Dublin, 1993).

Supplementary bibliography for second edition

D. E. Jordan, *Land and Popular Politics in Ireland, County Mayo from the Plantation to the Land War* (Cambridge 1994); D. A. Kerr, *'A Nation of Beggars'?, Priests, People, and Politics in Famine Ireland, 1846-1852* (Oxford 1994); C. Kinealy, *This Great Calamity, The Irish Famine 1845-52* (Dublin 1994); H. Litton, *The Irish Famine, An Illustrated History* (Dublin 1994); D. Mullan, ed. *'A Glimmer of Light', An Overview of Great Hunger Commemorative Events in Ireland and throughout the World* (Dublin 1995); C. Ó'Gráda, *Ireland, A New Economic History 1780-1939* (Oxford 1994); R. J. Scally, *The End of Hidden Ireland, Rebellion, Famine, and Emigration* (Oxford and New York 1995); A. Somerville (ed. K. D. M. Snell) *Letters from Ireland during the Famine of 1847* (Dublin 1994); W. E. Vaughan, *Landlords and Tenants in Mid-Victorian Ireland* (Oxford 1994).